Contents

The Ultimate Book of Baby Names

2022 – Updated Version

- By Clint Hammerstrike

Introduction

Choosing a baby name can be a tough gig. Experience has taught me that what one person thinks is a perfectly respectable name for a child can be another person's worst nightmare.

To make matters worse the name that you choose to give your child will follow them for their entire life. It will be the name that they are called from birth through to old age. This responsibility should not be taken lightly.

There are so many names that one could possibly choose. So how can one even begin to find that perfect name that will set your child up for a happy and successful life. If only there was a way to simplify the whole process.

Well thankfully for you, you have picked up a copy of "The Ultimate Book of Baby Names".

This book will help you sort your Aaron from your Zachariah, your Abby from your Zoe and a whole host of names in between.

Things to consider

You must love your name:

Liking a name is not enough. This is going to be the name that your child carries with them for the rest of their lives. It will be a name that you will use every day of every week of every year. If you are uncertain of it during the pregnancy it is unlikely that come labour day you will be any keener on the name.

Spelling:

In order to reduce the confusion and simplify the process of using this book, every effort has been taken to remove the many duplicate ways of spelling a name. Many books containing thousands upon thousands of names are padded out with several variations of the same name. For instance, the name Hayley can be spelt in the following ways: Hailee, Hailey, Haily, Hailie, Haley, Haleigh, Haylee and Hayleigh! For the purposes of this book the author has taken a choice on a single or limited variety of spelling for a name. If you like the sound of a name you can always search for alternative spellings of that name if you do not like the composition in this book.

Make sure the name is suitable and appropriate:

When choosing a name, it is important to remember the context that you are going to have to use it. This is a name that you are going to have to call out across a supermarket and have read out on school registers.

It is also important to remember that certain names have certain slang connotations. You should also consider the full name your child will have when combining their first name with second name and surname. You only need to have seen a few episodes of "The Simpsons" to know that there are some combinations you should avoid. These include:

- Seymour Butts
- Al Caholic
- Harry Chinn

If you are in doubt about a name combination it is well worth using the internet to do a little research. It is also worth considering whether your chosen name translates well into other languages. Some names have very different meanings in other languages. It is also worth considering what your child's potential initials could spell out. You may want to avoid naming your child **C**arol **R**achel **A**my **P**arkinson!

It is also worth checking out whether the country where you will be registering your child have any restrictions when it comes to names. Some banned names across the world include:

- Nutella (France)
- Akuma – Meaning Devil (Japan)
- Anal (New Zealand)
- Robocop (Mexico)
- BRFXXCCXXMNPCCCLLLMMNPRXV CLMNCKSSQLBB11116 (Sweden)
- Chow Tow – Meaning smelly head (Malaysia)

Shortening of names:

It is well worth considering how you feel about the shortening of names. Some shortening of names includes:

- Thomas – Tom
- Maximillian – Max
- Stephanie – Steph
- Catherine – Cathy
- Robert – Rob
- William – Will
- Eleanor – Ellie
- Madeline – Maddy

The likelihood is that your child will often be called by the shortened form of their name by their peers. If you do not like a shortened variation of your chosen name this does not have to be a critical issue but it is worth considering.

Check your name compliments your surname:

Whilst you will rarely use your child's first name, second name (if relevant) and surname together it is important that the they complement each other. As you work through this book do consider whether you like the flow and cadence of the name.

Check the popular names:

Every year many lists are compiled of the most popular names for boys and girls in different countries. In the UK in 2022 the top 10 popular name for boys were:

1. Noah
2. Liam
3. Oliver
4. Elijah
5. Mateo
6. Lucas
7. James

8. Levi
9. Grayson
10. Daniel

The 2022 top 10 names for girls were:

1. Emma
2. Amelia
3. Olivia
4. Ava
5. Luna
6. Mia
7. Ella
8. Sophia
9. Charlotte
10. Isabella

It is worthwhile taking a look at these lists as it gives you a good idea of the names of the children your child is likely to grow up with. There is a good chance that if you have a child in 2022 they could end up in a school class with a couple of girls and boys called Noah and Emma. Do not let this put you off using a name if you love it, just be aware that others may love it too.

Baby Name Meanings:

For some people a name with meaning is important. Thankfully the internet is littered with sites where you can look up the meaning of a name. For the purposes of this book we have not included the meaning of names because across the course of a person's life the choice of name is more important than the meaning of the name. Therefore, I encourage you to focus on choosing the name that you like the most rather than the name you feel confers the greatest meaning. In reality, when your child steps into a boardroom or scores the winning goal in a world cup people will know their name not the meaning of their name.

Sharing names and ignoring the haters!

An important decision faces you during the course of the pregnancy – do you tell people your baby name? If so, who? Whether you decide to share your baby name choices is up to you. However, if you decide to tell friends and family your choice of name you are opening yourself up to their opinions which may or may not be welcome. By sharing a name, you run the risk of having a name that you love tarnished by their opinion or experience. People are more likely to be forthcoming with negative opinions before the baby is born. Once your bundle of joy arrives people are unlikely to be critical.

Enjoy yourself

Do not let choosing a name become a burden. That I am aware of there are very few adults walking around this earth without a name because their parents could not decide on a name. Instead let this be an opportunity for fun and exploration. This is why this book has been set out like a competitive game. Enjoy comparing and contrasting names until you come up with your winner.

How to use this book?

To help you during this exciting period in your life. I have suggested some guidelines for how best to help you work through this book.

- There are two sections to this book. The first section contains names for a daughter the second contains names for a son.

- Each section is split Chapters A through to Z

- For each question you will be faced with an initial question:

  ❖ Would you rather name your son/daughter x OR y?

- Your first task is to make a decision on which of these names you prefer.

- Once you have decided on which name you prefer you can move onto the next name on the list.

- You must then ask yourself the question would rather name your son/daughter the name you chose in the previous round or the new name.

- Once you reach the end of the chapter write your favourite name from that chapter against the corresponding letter on the top name list.

- Once you have completed all 26 chapters you will have sorted through hundreds of names to reach your top 26 names. From this list you can choose the winner!

Gorgeous names for girls

A	
B	
C	
D	
E	
F	
G	
H	
I	
J	
K	
L	
M	
N	
O	
P	

Q	
R	
S	
T	
U	
V	
W	
X	
Y	
Z	

And the Winner is

....

A

Would you rather name your daughter

Aaliyah OR Abby?

- ❖ Abela

- ❖ Abigail

- ❖ Abijah

- ❖ Ada

- ❖ Adaline

- ❖ Addison

- ❖ Adelaide

- ❖ Adele

- ❖ Adeline

- ❖ Adora

- ❖ Adrianna

- ❖ Adrienne

- ❖ Afia

- ❖ Agatha

- ❖ Agda

- ❖ Agnes

- ❖ Aida

- ❖ Aileen

- ❖ Aimee

- ❖ Ainsley

- ❖ Aisha

- ❖ Aislinn

- ❖ Aiyana

- ❖ Akhila

- ❖ Alana

- ❖ Aleena

- ❖ Alejandra

- ❖ Alena

- ❖ Alex

- ❖ Alexa

- ❖ Alexandra

- ❖ Alexandria

- ❖ Alexia

- ❖ Alexis

- ❖ Alianna
- ❖ Alice
- ❖ Alicia
- ❖ Alisha
- ❖ Alison
- ❖ Allegra
- ❖ Allie
- ❖ Alyssa
- ❖ Amanda
- ❖ Amaya

- ❖ Amber

- ❖ Amelia

- ❖ Amelie

- ❖ Amina

- ❖ Amy

- ❖ Amya

- ❖ Ana

- ❖ Anabella

- ❖ Anabelle

- ❖ Anastasia

- ❖ Anaya

- ❖ Andi

- ❖ Andrea

- ❖ Angel

- ❖ Angela

- ❖ Angelica

- ❖ Angelina

- ❖ Angelique

- ❖ Angie

- ❖ Anika

- ❖ Ann

- ❖ Anna

- ❖ Annabel

- ❖ Annabella

- ❖ Annalee

- ❖ Annie

- ❖ Annushka

- ❖ Anotonia

- ❖ April

- ❖ Arabella

- ❖ Arden

- ❖ Aria

- ❖ Arianna

- ❖ Ariel

- ❖ Arielle

- ❖ Arlene

- ❖ Arya

- ❖ Ashley

- ❖ Ashlyn

- ❖ Asia

- ❖ Aspen

- ❖ Astrid

- ❖ Athena

- ❖ Aubree

- ❖ Aubriella

- ❖ Auburn

- ❖ Audrey

- ❖ Aurelia

- ❖ Aurora

- ❖ Autumn

- ❖ Ava

- ❖ Avalyn

- ❖ Avery

- ❖ Avianna

- ❖ Aya

- ❖ Ayla

- ❖ Ayleen

❖ Azalea

❖ Azaria

B

Would you rather name your daughter

Bailey OR Barbara?

- ❖ Beatrice

- ❖ Becky

- ❖ Belen

- ❖ Bella

- ❖ Bernadette

- ❖ Bertha

- ❖ Bethany

- ❖ Betsy

- ❖ Betty

- ❖ Beverly

- ❖ Beyonce

- ❖ Bianca

- ❖ Billie

- ❖ Blair

- ❖ Blanche

- ❖ Blake

- ❖ Blakely

- ❖ Blossom

- ❖ Bobbie

- ❖ Bonnie

- ❖ Bree

- ❖ Brenda

- ❖ Bria

- ❖ Brianna

- ❖ Briar

- ❖ Bridget

- ❖ Briony

- ❖ Brittany

- ❖ Brooke

- ❖ Brooklyn

- ❖ Brynn

- ❖ Buffy

C

Would you rather name your daughter

Cadence OR Caitlin?

- ❖ Caitriona

- ❖ Callie

- ❖ Camellia

- ❖ Cameron

- ❖ Camilla

- ❖ Camille
- ❖ Candace
- ❖ Cara
- ❖ Carey
- ❖ Carissa
- ❖ Carla
- ❖ Carly
- ❖ Carmella
- ❖ Carmen
- ❖ Carolina

- Caroline

- Carolyn

- Carrie

- Casey

- Cassandra

- Cassidy

- Catalina

- Catherine

- Cecelia

- Cecily

- ❖ Celeste

- ❖ Celine

- ❖ Ceren

- ❖ Chanel

- ❖ Chantal

- ❖ Charity

- ❖ Charley

- ❖ Charlene

- ❖ Charlize

- ❖ Charlotte

- ❖ Chelsea

- ❖ Cherish

- ❖ Cheryl

- ❖ Chloe

- ❖ Christina

- ❖ Christine

- ❖ Christy

- ❖ Ciara

- ❖ Cindy

- ❖ Claire

- ❖ Clara

- ❖ Clarissa

- ❖ Claudia

- ❖ Clementine

- ❖ Cleo

- ❖ Colleen

- ❖ Collins

- ❖ Cora

- ❖ Coraline

- ❖ Cordelia

- ❖ Corinne

- ❖ Courtney

- ❖ Crystal

- ❖ Cybill

- ❖ Cynthia

D

Would you rather name your daughter

Dahlia OR Daisy?

- ❖ Dakota

- ❖ Dallas

- ❖ Dana

- ❖ Danielle

- ❖ Danna

- Daphne

- Darcey

- Darlene

- Davina

- Dawn

- Deborah

- Deirdre

- Delaney

- Delilah

- ❖ Delta

- ❖ Demi

- ❖ Denise

- ❖ Desiree

- ❖ Destiny

- ❖ Devon

- ❖ Diamanda

- ❖ Diana

- ❖ Dido

- ❖ Divina

- ❖ Dixie

- ❖ Dolly

- ❖ Dominique

- ❖ Dona

- ❖ Dora

- ❖ Dorothy

- ❖ Drew

- ❖ Drucilla

- ❖ Dylan

E

Would you rather name your daughter

Ebony OR Eden?

- ❖ Edith

- ❖ Edna

- ❖ Edwina

- ❖ Effie

- ❖ Eileen

- ❖ Elaina

- ❖ Elaine

- ❖ Elanor

- ❖ Electra

- ❖ Eliana

- ❖ Elisa

- ❖ Elise

- ❖ Elizabeth

- ❖ Ella

- ❖ Ellen

- ❖ Ellie

- ❖ Elliott

- ❖ Ellis

- ❖ Ellison

- ❖ Eloise

- ❖ Elsa

- ❖ Emelia

- ❖ Emerie

- ❖ Emerson

- ❖ Emilie

- ❖ Emily

- ❖ Emma

- ❖ Emmeline

- ❖ Emmy

- ❖ Enid

- ❖ Erica

- ❖ Erin

- ❖ Esme

- ❖ Esmeralda

- ❖ Estelle

- ❖ Esther

- ❖ Eugine

- ❖ Eva

- ❖ Evangeline

- ❖ Eve

- ❖ Evelyn

- ❖ Everly

- ❖ Evie

❖ Evonne

F

Would you rather name your daughter

Faith OR Fanny?

- ❖ Farrah

- ❖ Fatima

- ❖ Faye

- ❖ Felicity

- ❖ Fenella

- ❖ Fern

- ❖ Fergie

- ❖ Fifi

- ❖ Filomena

- ❖ Finley

- ❖ Fiona

- ❖ Flavia

- ❖ Flora

- ❖ Florence

- ❖ Frances

- ❖ Francesca

- ❖ Frankie

- ❖ Frieda

- ❖ Freya

- ❖ Frida

G

Would you rather name your daughter

Gabi OR Gabriella?

❖ Gabrielle

❖ Gail

❖ Gaynor

❖ Gemma

❖ Genevieve

- ❖ Georgette

- ❖ Georgia

- ❖ Geraldine

- ❖ Gertrude

- ❖ Gia

- ❖ Giana

- ❖ Gillian

- ❖ Gina

- ❖ Ginny

- ❖ Giselle

- ❖ Gisela

- ❖ Giuliana

- ❖ Gladys

- ❖ Glenda

- ❖ Gloria

- ❖ Grace

- ❖ Gracelyn

- ❖ Gracie

- ❖ Greta

- ❖ Gretchen

- ❖ Gretel

- ❖ Guinevere

- ❖ Gwen

- ❖ Gwendolyn

H

Would you rather name your daughter

Hadleigh OR Hailey?

- ❖ Hallie

- ❖ Hana

- ❖ Hannah

- ❖ Harley

- ❖ Harlow

- ❖ Harmony

- ❖ Harper

- ❖ Harriet

- ❖ Hattie

- ❖ Haven

- ❖ Hayden

- ❖ Hayley

- ❖ Hazel

- ❖ Heather

- ❖ Heaven

- ❖ Heidi

- ❖ Helen

- ❖ Helena

- ❖ Helga

- ❖ Henrietta

- ❖ Hilary

- ❖ Holly

- ❖ Hope

I

Would you rather name your daughter

Ida Or Ileana?

- ❖ Imogen

- ❖ Ingrid

- ❖ India

- ❖ Indiana

- ❖ Indigo

- ❖ Ireland

- ❖ Irene

- ❖ Iris

- ❖ Isa

- ❖ Isabel

- ❖ Isabella

- ❖ Isobel

- ❖ Isla

- ❖ Ivanna

- ❖ Ivory

❖ Ivy

J

Would you rather name your daughter

Jacqueline OR Jada?

- ❖ Jade

- ❖ Jamie

- ❖ Janelle

- ❖ Jasmine

- ❖ Jayde

- ❖ Jayden

- ❖ Jemma

- ❖ Jenna

- ❖ Jennifer

- ❖ Jenny

- ❖ Jessica

- ❖ Jessie

- ❖ Jewel

- ❖ Jillian

❖ Joanna
❖ Jocelynn

❖ Johanna

❖ Jolie

❖ Jordan

❖ Joselyn

❖ Josephine

❖ Josie

❖ Journey

❖ Joy

- ❖ Joyce
- ❖ Judith

- ❖ Julia

- ❖ Julianna

- ❖ Julie

- ❖ Juliet

- ❖ Julieta

- ❖ June

- ❖ Juniper

- ❖ Justice

K

Would you rather name your daughter

Kailey OR Kaitlynn?

- ❖ Kallie

- ❖ Kamila

- ❖ Kara

- ❖ Karen

- ❖ Karla

- ❖ Kate

- ❖ Kathryn

- ❖ Katie

- ❖ Kayleigh

- ❖ Keira

- ❖ Kelly

- ❖ Kelsey

- ❖ Kendra

- ❖ Kenley

- ❖ Kennedy

- ❖ Kensley

- ❖ Kenya

- ❖ Kenzie

- ❖ Khaleesi

- ❖ Kloe

- ❖ Kiara

- ❖ Kiera

- ❖ Kimberly

- ❖ Kira

- ❖ Kora

- ❖ Korsi

- ❖ Kristen

- ❖ Kristina

- ❖ Kyla

- ❖ Kylie

L

Would you rather name your daughter

Lacey OR Laila?

- ❖ Lainey

- ❖ Lana

- ❖ Landry

- ❖ Lara

- ❖ Laura

- ❖ Laurel

- ❖ Lauren

- ❖ Layla

- ❖ Lea

- ❖ Leah

- ❖ Leanna

- ❖ Lennon

- ❖ Lennox

- ❖ Leona

- ❖ Leslie

- ❖ Lexi

- ❖ Lia

- ❖ Libby

- ❖ Liberty

- ❖ Liliana

- ❖ Lilian

- ❖ Lily

- ❖ Linda

- ❖ Lindsay

- ❖ Lisa
- ❖ Liv
- ❖ Logan
- ❖ Lola
- ❖ Lorelai
- ❖ Louisa
- ❖ Lucia
- ❖ Luciana
- ❖ Lucille

- ❖ Lucy

- ❖ Luna

- ❖ Lydia

- ❖ Lyla

M

Would you rather name your daughter

Mabel OR Macie?

❖ Mackenzie

❖ Madalynn

❖ Maddison

❖ Madeline

❖ Mae

- ❖ Maeve

- ❖ Maggie

- ❖ Magnolia

- ❖ Maia

- ❖ Maisie

- ❖ Makayla

- ❖ Makenna

- ❖ Malaya

- ❖ Maleah

- ❖ Malia

- ❖ Mallory

- ❖ Mara

- ❖ Margaret

- ❖ Margot

- ❖ Maria

- ❖ Mariam

- ❖ Mariana

- ❖ Marie

- ❖ Marina

- ❖ Marissa

- ❖ Marjorie

- ❖ Marlee

- ❖ Martha

- ❖ Mary

- ❖ Maryam

- ❖ Matilda

- ❖ Maya

- ❖ Mckinley

- ❖ Meadow

- ❖ Megain

- ❖ Melanie

- ❖ Melissa

- ❖ Melody

- ❖ Meredith

- ❖ Mia

- ❖ Michaela

- ❖ Michelle

- ❖ Mila

- ❖ Millie

- ❖ Miranda

- ❖ Miriam

- ❖ Molly

- ❖ Monica

- ❖ Morgan

- ❖ Moriah

N

Would you rather name your daughter

Nadia OR Nadine?

❖ Nala

❖ Nancy

❖ Naomi

❖ Natalie

❖ Natasha

- ❖ Nathalia

- ❖ Naya

- ❖ Nayeli

- ❖ Nevaeh

- ❖ Nia

- ❖ Nicole

- ❖ Nikita

- ❖ Nikki

- ❖ Nina

- ❖ Noa

- ❖ Nola

- ❖ Nora

- ❖ Norah

- ❖ Norma

- ❖ Nova

O

Would you rather name your daughter

Oakley OR Oceana?

- ❖ Octavia

- ❖ Odelia

- ❖ Odysseia

- ❖ Oksana

- ❖ Olga

- ❖ Olive

- ❖ Olivia

- ❖ Olympia

- ❖ Opel

- ❖ Ophelia

- ❖ Oprah

- ❖ Oriana

- ❖ Oriel

P

Would you rather name your daughter

Pamela OR Paige

- ❖ Paiselee

- ❖ Paloma

- ❖ Pam

- ❖ Pandora

- ❖ Paris

- ❖ Parker

- ❖ Patience

- ❖ Patricia

- ❖ Paula

- ❖ Paulina

- ❖ Payton

- ❖ Pearl

- ❖ Peggy

- ❖ Penelope

- ❖ Penny

- ❖ Persephonie

- ❖ Petra

- ❖ Peyton

- ❖ Phoebe

- ❖ Phoenix

- ❖ Phyllis

- ❖ Pia

- ❖ Piper

- ❖ Pippa

- ❖ Poppy

- ❖ Portia

- ❖ Priscilla

- ❖ Prudence

- ❖ Prunella

Q

Would you rather name your daughter

Qianru OR Quela?

- ❖ Quenby

- ❖ Queenie

- ❖ Quibilah

- ❖ Quies

- ❖ Quinby

- ❖ Quinlan

- ❖ Quinn

- ❖ Quinta

R

Would you rather name your daughter

Rachel OR Rachelle?

- ❖ Rae

- ❖ Raegan

- ❖ Raelyn

- ❖ Ramona

- ❖ Raquel

- ❖ Raven

- ❖ Rayna

- ❖ Reagan

- ❖ Rebecca

- ❖ Renee

- ❖ Reese

- ❖ Regina

- ❖ Rhea

- ❖ Rhianna

- ❖ Rhiannon

- ❖ Riley

- ❖ Ripley

- ❖ Rita

- ❖ River

- ❖ Roberta

- ❖ Robin

- ❖ Rory

- ❖ Rosa

- ❖ Rosalie

- ❖ Rosalind

- ❖ Rosanne

- ❖ Rose

- ❖ Rosemary

- ❖ Rosie

- ❖ Rowan

- ❖ Roxanne

- ❖ Ruby

- ❖ Ruth

- ❖ Ryan

❖ Rylan

S

Would you rather name your daughter

Sabrina OR Sadie?

- ❖ Saffron

- ❖ Sage

- ❖ Salma

- ❖ Samantha

- ❖ Samara

- Sapphire

- Sandra

- Sara

- Sarah

- Sasha

- Savannah

- Sawyer

- Scarlett

- Scout

- Selena

- ❖ Serena

- ❖ Serenity

- ❖ Shannon

- ❖ Sharon

- ❖ Shayla

- ❖ Sheena

- ❖ Sheila

- ❖ Shelby

- ❖ Shelley

❖ Sherry

❖ Shiloh

❖ Shirley

❖ Sidney

❖ Sienna

❖ Sierra

❖ Silvia

❖ Simone

❖ Sky

❖ Skylar

- ❖ Sofia

- ❖ Sonia

- ❖ Sophia

- ❖ Sophie

- ❖ Stacey

- ❖ Stella

- ❖ Stephanie

- ❖ Stevie

- ❖ Storm

- ❖ Sue

- ❖ Summer

- ❖ Susan

- ❖ Sutton

- ❖ Suzanne

- ❖ Sybil

- ❖ Sydney

- ❖ Sylvia

T

Would you rather name your daughter

Tabitha OR Tallulah?

- ❖ Tamara

- ❖ Tammy

- ❖ Tanya

- ❖ Tara

- ❖ Tasha

- ❖ Tatiana

- ❖ Taylor

- ❖ Tawny

- ❖ Tegan

- ❖ Teresa

- ❖ Tess

- ❖ Tessa

- ❖ Thea

- ❖ Theodora

- ❖ Tiana

- ❖ Tiffany

- ❖ Tina

- ❖ Tilly

- ❖ Toni

- ❖ Tori

- ❖ Tracy

- ❖ Trinity

- ❖ Trish

- ❖ Trisha

- ❖ Trudy

- ❖ Tyra

U

Would you rather name your daughter

Ualda OR Udele?

- ❖ Ulalia

- ❖ Uli

- ❖ Ulla

- ❖ Ulu

- ❖ Ulyana

- ❖ Uma

- ❖ Una

- ❖ Undine

- ❖ Unique

- ❖ Urbi

- ❖ Uri

- ❖ Ursa

- ❖ Ursula

- ❖ Usha

V

Would you rather name your daughter

Valentina OR Valencia?

- ❖ Valerie

- ❖ Vanessa

- ❖ Vega

- ❖ Venus

- ❖ Vera

- ❖ Verna

- ❖ Veronica

- ❖ Victoria

- ❖ Vienna

- ❖ Viola

- ❖ Violet

- ❖ Violetta

- ❖ Virginia

- ❖ Vivian

- ❖ Vivienne

Would you rather name your daughter

Wallis OR Wanda?

❖ Wendy

❖ Westley

❖ Whitley

❖ Wilhemina

❖ Wilma

❖ Winona

- ❖ Winnie

- ❖ Winnifred

- ❖ Witney

- ❖ Willow

- ❖ Winter

- ❖ Wren

X

Would you rather name your daughter

Xabrina OR Xanthe?

❖ Xavierre

❖ Xena

❖ Xenia

❖ Xia

❖ Xio

- ❖ Xiomara

- ❖ Xuxa

- ❖ Xyliana

- ❖ Xylona

Y

Would you rather name your daughter

Yana OR Yara?

- ❖ Yasmin

- ❖ Yesenia

- ❖ Yoana

- ❖ Yolanda

- ❖ Ysabelle

- ❖ Yulia

- ❖ Yvette

- ❖ Yvonne

Z

Would you rather name your daughter

Zaidee OR Zanthe?

- ❖ Zara

- ❖ Zarah

- ❖ Zahara

- ❖ Zelda

- ❖ Zella

- ❖ Zendaya

- ❖ Zephyr

- ❖ Zeta

- ❖ Zia

- ❖ Zoe

- ❖ Zoelle

- ❖ Zoey

- ❖ Zofie

- ❖ Zola

Beautiful names for boys

A	
B	
C	
D	
E	
F	
G	
H	
I	
J	
K	
L	
M	
N	
O	
P	
Q	

R	
S	
T	
U	
V	
W	
X	
Y	
Z	

And the Winner is

·······································

A

Would you rather name your son

Aaden OR Aaron?

- ❖ Abdullah

- ❖ Abel

- ❖ Abraham

- ❖ Achilles

- ❖ Adam

- ❖ Aden

- ❖ Adonis

- ❖ Adrian

- ❖ Agustin

- ❖ Ahmad

- ❖ Alan

- ❖ Albert

- ❖ Alberto

- ❖ Alden

- ❖ Aldo

- ❖ Alec

- ❖ Alessandro

- ❖ Alexander

- ❖ Alexis

- ❖ Alfonso

- ❖ Alfred

- ❖ Aldredo

- ❖ Ali

- ❖ Allan

- ❖ Alonson

- ❖ Alvaro

- ❖ Alvin

- ❖ Amir

- ❖ Amos

- ❖ Anakin

- ❖ Anders

- ❖ Anderson

- ❖ Andre

- ❖ Andrew

- ❖ Angel

- ❖ Angelo

- ❖ Anthony

- ❖ Antoine

- ❖ Apollo

- ❖ Archer

- ❖ Arian

- ❖ Ariel

- ❖ Armani

- ❖ Arthur

- ❖ Asher

- ❖ Ashton

- ❖ Atlas

- ❖ Atticus

- ❖ Augustus

- ❖ Austin

- ❖ Avery

- ❖ Axel

- ❖ Ayden

B

Would you rather name your son

Beau OR Benjamin?

- ❖ Benson

- ❖ Bentley

- ❖ Benton

- ❖ Billy

- ❖ Bishop

- ❖ Blaine

- ❖ Blake

- ❖ Bo

- ❖ Bobby

- ❖ Boden

- ❖ Boston

- ❖ Bradley

- ❖ Brady

- ❖ Braiden

- ❖ Brandon

- ❖ Branson

- ❖ Braydon

- ❖ Brendan

- ❖ Brentley

- ❖ Brett

- ❖ Brian

- ❖ Brice

- ❖ Brock

- ❖ Brodie

- ❖ Bronson
- ❖ Brooks
- ❖ Bruce
- ❖ Bruno
- ❖ Bryant
- ❖ Byron

C

Would you rather name your son

Cade OR Cain?

- ❖ Caleb

- ❖ Callan

- ❖ Callum

- ❖ Calvin

- ❖ Cameron

- ❖ Cannon

- ❖ Carl

- ❖ Carlos

- ❖ Carson

- ❖ Carter

- ❖ Casey

- ❖ Cash

- ❖ Cassius

- ❖ Cedric

- ❖ Cesar

- ❖ Chace

- ❖ Chad

- ❖ Chandler

- ❖ Channing

- ❖ Charles

- ❖ Charlie

- ❖ Chase

- ❖ Chevy

- ❖ Chris

- ❖ Christian

- ❖ Christopher

- ❖ Clark

- ❖ Clayton

- ❖ Clint

- ❖ Clinton

- ❖ Clyde

- ❖ Cody

- ❖ Cohen

- ❖ Colby

- ❖ Cole

- ❖ Coleman

- ❖ Colin

- ❖ Colt

- ❖ Connor

- ❖ Conrad

- ❖ Cooper

- ❖ Corey

- ❖ Craig

- ❖ Crew

- ❖ Cristian

- ❖ Cristiano

- ❖ Crosby

- ❖ Cruz

- ❖ Cullen

- ❖ Curtis

- ❖ Cyrus

D

Would you rather name your son

Dakota OR Dallas?

- ❖ Damari

- ❖ Damien

- ❖ Damon

- ❖ Daniel

- ❖ Danny

- ❖ Dante

- ❖ Dariel

- ❖ Darius

- ❖ Darell

- ❖ Darren

- ❖ Darwin

- ❖ Dash

- ❖ Davian

- ❖ David

- ❖ Davis

- ❖ Dawson

- ❖ Dax

- ❖ Dayton

- ❖ Deacon

- ❖ Dean

- ❖ Deandre

- ❖ Deangelo

- ❖ Dennis

- ❖ Denver

- ❖ Derek

- ❖ Deshawn

- ❖ Desmond

- ❖ Devin

- ❖ Dexter

- ❖ Diego

- ❖ Dillon

- ❖ Dimitri

- ❖ Dominic

- ❖ Donald

- ❖ Donovan

- ❖ Dorian

- ❖ Douglas

- ❖ Drake

- ❖ Drew

- ❖ Duke

- ❖ Duncan

- ❖ Dustin

- ❖ Dwayne

❖ Dylan

E

Would you rather name your son

Eddie OR Edgar?

- ❖ Edison

- ❖ Eduardo

- ❖ Edward

- ❖ Edwin

- ❖ Eli

- ❖ Elias

- ❖ Elijah

- ❖ Elliot

- ❖ Ellis

- ❖ Emanuel

- ❖ Emerson

- ❖ Emery

- ❖ Emiliano

- ❖ Emmanuel

- ❖ Emmett

- ❖ Enrique

- ❖ Enzo

- ❖ Ephraim

- ❖ Eric

- ❖ Ernest

- ❖ Ernesto

- ❖ Ethan

- ❖ Eugene

- ❖ Evan

- ❖ Everett

- ❖ Ezekiel

- ❖ Ezra

F

Would you rather name your son

Fabian OR Felipe?

- ❖ Fabian

- ❖ Fabio

- ❖ Fabrice

- ❖ Fallon

- ❖ Felix

- ❖ Fernando

- ❖ Ferris

- ❖ Finley

- ❖ Finian

- ❖ Finnegan

- ❖ Fisher

- ❖ Fletcher

- ❖ Flint

- ❖ Floyd

- ❖ Flynn

- ❖ Ford

- ❖ Forrest

- ❖ Francis

- ❖ Francisco

- ❖ Franco

- ❖ Frank

- ❖ Frankie

- ❖ Franklin

- ❖ Fraser

- ❖ Freddy

❖ Frederick

❖ Fritz

G

Would you rather name your son

Gabe OR Gabriel?

- ❖ Gale

- ❖ Gareth

- ❖ Garrett

- ❖ Garry

- ❖ Garrison

- ❖ Gavin

- ❖ George

- ❖ Gerald

- ❖ Gerard

- ❖ Gianni

- ❖ Gibson

- ❖ Gideon

- ❖ Gil

- ❖ Gilbert

- ❖ Giovani

- ❖ Glenn

- ❖ Gordon

- ❖ Grady

- ❖ Graham

- ❖ Grant

- ❖ Grayson

- ❖ Gregory

- ❖ Grey

- ❖ Griffin

- ❖ Gus

❖ Gustavo

❖ Guy

H

Would you rather name your son

Haiden OR Hamilton?

- ❖ Hank

- ❖ Harley

- ❖ Harold

- ❖ Harper

- ❖ Harris

- ❖ Harrison

- ❖ Harry

- ❖ Harvey

- ❖ Hassan

- ❖ Hayden

- ❖ Hayes

- ❖ Heath

- ❖ Hector

- ❖ Hendrix

- ❖ Henrik

- ❖ Henry

- ❖ Herbert

- ❖ Horace

- ❖ Horatio

- ❖ Houston

- ❖ Howell

- ❖ Howie

- ❖ Hudson

- ❖ Hugh

❖ Hugo

❖ Hunter

❖ Huxley

I

Would you rather name your son

Ian OR Ibrahim?

- ❖ Idris

- ❖ Ignacio

- ❖ Ignatius

- ❖ Ignus

- ❖ Igor

❖ Ike

❖ Illias

❖ Immanuel

❖ Ira

❖ Isaac

❖ Isaiah

❖ Ishmael

❖ Israel

❖ Ivan

J

Would you rather name your son

Jack OR Jackson?

- ❖ Jacob

- ❖ Jake

- ❖ Jamal

- ❖ James

- ❖ Jamie

- ❖ Jared

- ❖ Jason

- ❖ Jasper

- ❖ Javier

- ❖ Javion

- ❖ Jay

- ❖ Jayden

- ❖ Jefferson

- ❖ Jeffrey

- ❖ Jeremiah

- ❖ Jeremy

- ❖ Jermaine

- ❖ Jerome

- ❖ Jerry

- ❖ Jessie

- ❖ Jimmy

- ❖ Joaquin

- ❖ Joe

- ❖ Joel

- ❖ Joey

- ❖ Johan

- ❖ John

- ❖ Johnathan

- ❖ Jon

- ❖ Jonael

- ❖ Jonah

- ❖ Jonas

- ❖ Jordan

- ❖ Jordy

- Jose

- Joseph

- Joshua

- Josiah

- Judah

- Jude

- Judson

- Julian

- Julio

- ❖ Julius

- ❖ Junior

- ❖ Justin

- ❖ Justus

K

Would you rather name your son

Kade OR Kaden?

- ❖ Kane

- ❖ Kai

- ❖ Kaleb

- ❖ Kane

- ❖ Karim

- ❖ Karson

- ❖ Kayden

- ❖ Keagan

- ❖ Keaton

- ❖ Keenan

- ❖ Keith

- ❖ Kellan

- ❖ Kelvin

- ❖ Ken

- ❖ Kendall

- ❖ Kendrick

- ❖ Kenneth

- ❖ Kenny

- ❖ Kevin

- ❖ Kian

- ❖ Kieran

- ❖ Killian

- ❖ King

- ❖ Kingsley

- ❖ Kingston

- ❖ Kipp

- ❖ Kirk

- ❖ Knox

- ❖ Kobe

- ❖ Kofi

- ❖ Konrad

- ❖ Kristoff

- ❖ Kurt

- ❖ Kye

❖ Kylan

❖ Kyle

L

Would you rather name your son

Lamar OR Lance?

- ❖ Landon

- ❖ Lane

- ❖ Larry

- ❖ Lawrence

- ❖ Lawson

- ❖ Layne

- ❖ Layton

- ❖ Lazarus

- ❖ Leandro

- ❖ Lee

- ❖ Leland

- ❖ Lennon

- ❖ Lennox

- ❖ Lenny

- ❖ Leo

- ❖ Leon

- ❖ Leonardo

- ❖ Leroy

- ❖ Levi

- ❖ Lewis

- ❖ Lex

- ❖ Liam

- ❖ Lincoln

- ❖ Linus

- ❖ Lionel

- ❖ Lochlan

- ❖ Logan

- ❖ London

- ❖ Lorenzo

- ❖ Louie

- ❖ Louis

- ❖ Lucas

- ❖ Lucian

- ❖ Luciano

- ❖ Lucius

- ❖ Luis

- ❖ Luke

- ❖ Lyndon

- ❖ Lyric

M

Would you rather name your son

Mack OR Madden?

- ❖ Maddox

- ❖ Magnus

- ❖ Maison

- ❖ Major

- ❖ Malachi

- ❖ Malcolm

- ❖ Malik

- ❖ Manuel

- ❖ Marc

- ❖ Marcel

- ❖ Marcelo

- ❖ Marco

- ❖ Marcus

- ❖ Mario

- ❖ Mark

- ❖ Marley

- ❖ Marlon

- ❖ Marshall

- ❖ Martin

- ❖ Marvin

- ❖ Mason

- ❖ Mateo

- ❖ Matias

- ❖ Matthew

- ❖ Maurice

- ❖ Max

- ❖ Maxim

- ❖ Maximillian

- ❖ Maximo

- ❖ Maximus

- ❖ Maxwell

- ❖ Memphis

- ❖ Micah

- ❖ Michael

- ❖ Miles

- ❖ Miller

- ❖ Milo

- ❖ Mitchell

- ❖ Mohamed

- ❖ Moises

- ❖ Morgan

- ❖ Moses

- ❖ Musa

❖ Mustafa

❖ Myles

N

Would you rather name your son

Nash OR Nathan?

- ❖ Nathaniel

- ❖ Nehemiah

- ❖ Neil

- ❖ Nelson

- ❖ Neville

- Newton

- Neymar

- Nicholas

- Nico

- Nigel

- Nikolai

- Niles

- Nixon

- Noah

- Noel

- ❖ Nolan

- ❖ Norbert

- ❖ Norman

- ❖ Norris

O

Would you rather name your son

Oakley OR Obadiah?

- ❖ Octavius

- ❖ Odell

- ❖ Odin

- ❖ Odysseus

- ❖ Olaf

- ❖ Oliver

- ❖ Omar

- ❖ Orion

- ❖ Orlando

- ❖ Orton

- ❖ Oscar

- ❖ Osmond

- ❖ Oswald

- ❖ Otis

- ❖ Otto

- ❖ Owen

- ❖ Oz

P

Would you rather name your son

Pablo OR Paris?

- ❖ Parker

- ❖ Pascal

- ❖ Patrick

- ❖ Paul

- ❖ Paulo

- ❖ Paxton

- ❖ Payton

- ❖ Pedro

- ❖ Percy

- ❖ Perry

- ❖ Peter

- ❖ Peyton

- ❖ Philip

- ❖ Phoenix

- ❖ Pierce

❖ Piers

❖ Pippin

❖ Porter

❖ Preston

❖ Prince

Q

Would you rather name your son

Quade OR Quentin?

❖ Quigley

❖ Quincy

❖ Quinlan

❖ Quinn

❖ Quintus

❖ Quinton

R

Would you rather name your son

Rafael OR Ramon?

- ❖ Randy

- ❖ Rashad

- ❖ Raul

- ❖ Ray

- ❖ Raymond

- ❖ Reagan

- ❖ Reede

- ❖ Reed

- ❖ Reginald

- ❖ Remington

- ❖ Remy

- ❖ Rene

- ❖ Reuben

- ❖ Rex

- ❖ Rey

- ❖ Rhys

- ❖ Riaan

- ❖ Ricardo

- ❖ Richard

- ❖ Ricky

- ❖ Riley

- ❖ River

- ❖ Robert

- ❖ Roberto

- ❖ Robin

- ❖ Rocco

- ❖ Rocky

- ❖ Rodney

- ❖ Rodrigo

- ❖ Roger

- ❖ Roland

- ❖ Rolando

- ❖ Roman

- ❖ Ronnie

- ❖ Rory

- ❖ Rowan

- ❖ Roy

- ❖ Royce

- ❖ Ruben

- ❖ Rudy

- ❖ Russell

- ❖ Ryan

- ❖ Ryder

❖ Rylan

S

Would you rather name your son

Sam OR Samir?

- ❖ Samson

- ❖ Samuel

- ❖ Santana

- ❖ Santiago

- ❖ Santino

- ❖ Santos

- ❖ Saul

- ❖ Sawyer

- ❖ Scott

- ❖ Scotty

- ❖ Seamus

- ❖ Sean

- ❖ Sebastian

- ❖ Serge

- ❖ Sergio

- ❖ Seth

- ❖ Shane

- ❖ Shaun

- ❖ Shay

- ❖ Sheldon

- ❖ Shiloh

- ❖ Sid

- ❖ Silas

- ❖ Simon

- ❖ Skelton

- ❖ Skylar

- ❖ Solomon

- ❖ Sonny

- ❖ Spencer

- ❖ Stan

- ❖ Stanley

- ❖ Stefan

- ❖ Stephen

- ❖ Sterling

- ❖ Steven

- ❖ Stewart

- ❖ Sullivan

T

Would you rather name your son

Tanner OR Tate?

- ❖ Tatum

- ❖ Taylor

- ❖ Terrance

- ❖ Terrell

- ❖ Terrence

- ❖ Terry

- ❖ Thaddeus

- ❖ Thatcher

- ❖ Theo

- ❖ Theodore

- ❖ Thiago

- ❖ Thomas

- ❖ Timothy

- ❖ Titan

- ❖ Titus

- ❖ Tobias

- ❖ Toby

- ❖ Todd

- ❖ Tomas

- ❖ Tommy

- ❖ Tony

- ❖ Travis

- ❖ Trent

- ❖ Trevor

❖ Trey

❖ Tristan

❖ Troy

❖ Truman

❖ Tucker

❖ Turner

❖ Tyler

❖ Tyrone

❖ Tyson

U

Would you rather name your son

Ugo OR Uli?

- ❖ Umberto

- ❖ Ungus

- ❖ Unwin

- ❖ Ura

- ❖ Urian

V

Would you rather name your son

Valentin OR Valentino?

- ❖ Van

- ❖ Vance

- ❖ Vaughn

- ❖ Vergil

- ❖ Vernon

- ❖ Vicente

- ❖ Victor

- ❖ Videl

- ❖ Vincent

- ❖ Vlad

- ❖ Vladimir

W

Would you rather name your son

Wade OR Walker?

- ❖ Walter

- ❖ Warren

- ❖ Watson

- ❖ Waylon

- ❖ Wayne

- ❖ Wendall

- ❖ Wes

- ❖ Wesley

- ❖ Westin

- ❖ Wilder

- ❖ Will

- ❖ Willard

- ❖ William

- ❖ Willis

- ❖ Wilson

- ❖ Winston

- ❖ Wyatt

Would you rather name your son

Xander OR Xavier?

- ❖ Xerxes

- ❖ Xenos

Y

Would you rather name your son

Yancy OR Yousef?

- ❖ Yancy

- ❖ Yousef

- ❖ York

- ❖ Yusuf

- ❖ Yura

- ❖ Yuri

Z

Would you rather name your son

Zacchaeus OR Zachariah?

- ❖ Zach

- ❖ Zachary

- ❖ Zahir

- ❖ Zander

- ❖ Zane

- ❖ Zavier

❖ Zebadiah

❖ Zechariah

❖ Zephaniah

Success

You have now reached the end of the book. Hopefully you managed to work through the contents of this book and select a name that you liked for each letter. From those 26 options I hope that you managed to choose a name that you absolutely love.

If not give yourself a few days and then then try again, it is amazing how a fresh perspective can change your opinion on a name.

Whatever name you finally selected we want to wish you every blessing and happiness for the birth of your child.

Made in the USA
Coppell, TX
31 July 2022

80699133R00132